a lonely world

and other poems

HIMANSHU GOEL

ALSO BY HIMANSHU GOEL

A Rational Boy in Love
52 Laws of Love
In Real Life
Swipe Left
The Nomad Who Stole my Heart
The Woman Who Saved my Life

a lonely world

and other poems

HIMANSHU GOEL

KALAMOS LITERARY SERVICES LLP

Kalamos Literary Services LLP
Email: info@kalamos.co.in | editorial@kalamos.co.in

Published in 2023
by
Kalamos Literary Services
ISBN- 978-93-91142-67-4

A Lonely World and Other Poems
Himanshu Goel

Typeset in Kalamos Literary Services LLP

Print and bound in India.

ACKNOWLEDGEMENT

Thank you to my parents, brother, and sister-in-law for their support.

Thank you to my wife for her support and the amazing illustrations in this book.

Dedicated to all the people who
have ever felt lonely in their life.

INTRODUCTION

Read these poems in the times you feel lonely, when the warm blanket is unable to provide you the comfort that you are used to.
Read these poems when you feel anxious, when even little thoughts feel like the weight of the world is upon you.
Read these poems in the times you feel most vulnerable.
Read these poems and know
that you are not alone in your loneliness.

"don't feel lonely
the entire universe is inside you"
Rumi

I

A Lonely World

vulnerability

isn't it strange
how afraid
we are to admit
just how lonely
and lost we are
how we long
to talk, to meet?

isn't it strange
how our fear
of vulnerability
is bigger than
our fear of being alone?

the loneliest places in the world

her friends try
to drag her to the
college party
where all the
hip crowd hangs out
but she'd rather be alone
and watch the sunset

for her clubs and concerts
were the loneliest places
in the world.

deep blue

she had a
deep blue loneliness
inside of her
the kind that
sneaks up on you
when you least expect it
the kind of loneliness
no other man or woman
     can cure

the kind of loneliness
that could only be cured
     from within.

a lonely world

it's a lonely world
and I'm a lonely boy
my only friend is
a lonely girl
she belongs to
another world
another universe
she exists only
on the small faded
screen of my smartphone

it's a lonely world
I'm a lonely boy
and there are countless
other lonely souls
just like mine.

don't ignore him

he is used to
being ignored
by his
friends
family
folks
in his neighbourhood
in the school
he wonders
how long
till someone notices
till someone listens

he is used to being ignored
and if you are reading this
don't ignore it, don't ignore him.

last man on the bench

I often go
to the park
across my home
where sits a man
on the bench
the last person
on this earth
who still talks to me
he's old
and when he's gone
I hope I still have
someone to go to.

pretending

look at us all
pretending to be
not broken
not knowing
we hold
the parts
to fix each other.

in this moment

I have been
alone all my life
without a family
without a friend
without a stranger

but in this moment
just for this
tiny fraction of time
I wish I wasn't lonely
I wish I had someone
with me.

love of a lonely soul

when I talk of love
I talk about
the love of a lonely soul

the one who
loves so strong
stronger than anyone
else in the world
but is too lonely
and afraid
to ever show it.

the highway

he had no one
only his car,
an empty road and
the highway to keep him company.

a sadness you'll never know

those who spend their nights
in halls full of smiling faces

those who have experienced
all the joys and
pleasures of the world

how could they ever know
what's it like to be me

let it be
a lullaby of the lonely
a sadness
they will never know

and I'll
not have it
any other way.

a lullaby of the lonely

let me sing you a lullaby
unlike any other

the kind in the
voice of the one
you love

the kind you have
never heard before
and never going
to hear again

the kind that puts
you to sleep with dreams
of places far away
and people close by

let me sing you
the lullaby of the lonely.

colour of loneliness

they say it's like
the blues and greys
of faded skies
and empty rooms

the black of the night
and the white of the morning
a painting of pastel
on crumpled paper

if only it was
as easy to describe
as a shade

no matter how
many times I tried

her loneliness
had no colour.

the only ally

they make fun
of me for making
fun of situations
that are not meant
to be joked about

they don't know
what's it like to be
defeated again and again
by life and there's
nothing to smile about
and humour is the
only ally you
have left.

this (battle) is personal

you have held my hand
a hundred times
and walked with me
on a thousand roads
but this one is different

this battle is personal
this journey is mine
I know you stood by me
and you will stand by me
long after this passes us by
but just this once
I must fight alone.

comfort zone

the places that
were supposed to be
my comfort zones
was where I felt
the most uncomfortable.

tsunami

keep away from me
I have become a disaster
in human form
with little earthquakes
deep in my soul
and a tsunami
on the shore
of my skin.

the periphery of the lonely

you can find
art in the periphery
of the lonely
the lit window
in a sea of dark
the sound
of careless footsteps
in the middle of night
tread with care
in the periphery
of the lonely.

self portrait

I took a photo
of mine
upside down
turned around
click click click
all the lights
all the angles
I took a photo
of mine
no lights
no filters
no alterations
straight into
the lens
looked the stranger

I took so many photos
of mine
but the person
in portraits
was not me.

an inconvenient truth

the sad truth
about our world
is that all of us
get lonely
but too few
have the courage
to say it out loud.

II

A Lonely Sleep

3 a.m

isn't it strange
that all the dreamers
are up at 3 am
some by choice
some by fate

isn't it strange
that all the dreamers
find big dreams
in little pockets of sleep?

a familiar stranger

I am familiar
with the dark
corners of the bed
that only appear
when the clock strikes
four in the morning

the bed, the pillows
the sheets and
the sounds
of the night
I am familiar with all of them
but sleep, sleep is still a stranger.

numb

I can't sleep
without something
playing in the background
a song, music, something
to numb my mind
and take me away from reality.

galaxy of thoughts

thousands of
thoughts
swirl around
in the galaxy
of her mind but
she struggles
she struggles to
share even a
single one.

ceiling

they
bestow us
with wings
glorious
than the
world has ever known
bless us with
wings more real
than flesh has ever felt

but how far can we really fly
when we look up and see
nothing beyond the grey ceiling.

dreams

I have a strange
fascination with dreams
the kind of ones
that come at
four in the night
sneak up to you
and hit you
like a gunshot
to the heart

I sometimes wonder
if these dreams
are showing me
what things
could have been
and maybe
what life is
for another version
of me in another world.

beneath the stars

is there no one
left in this new world
that can lie down
beneath the
stars with me
and sing me old songs?

the boy on the floor

let me tell
you about this
boy who used
to sleep on the
floor because he
was too afraid
of satin sheets
and the night above

he always kept
his dreams grounded
too afraid to take off

he used to sleep
on the cold hard floor
afraid that once he left for the skies
his feet would
never touch the ground.

bonfire of dreams

for every dream fulfilled
there are a million
left up in the flames
some almost make it
some halfway
and some don't even
get the chance to start.

madness beckons

madness beckons
for me to stay up
at hours past midnight
sacrifice my sleep
and sanity
for one more time
as the night
gets deeper

madness beckons
to me
one last time.

no dreams

I sleep but have no dreams
wake up and weep and wonder
what it would be like
to imagine
have dreams like everyone else
finally sleep
with something
to look forward to.

a night in the heavens

you mistook
stars reflected in a pond
for a night in the heavens

you mistook a
spark in the grass
for the light of the skies

you mistook
a glass of water
for a swim in the ocean

you mistook
a sign of affection
as the love of your life.

III

Lonely Together

origami

my paper skin
folds like origami
to your touch
like two paper boats
in a storm
it folds
twists and breaks
until it all washes away.

broken clocks

remember the time
we used to take
long walks
in small towns
and pretend
our clocks
were broken.

little fingers

and I cling
to you by my
little finger
hoping some
of you
rub off
on me
and fix my
broken parts.

the girl who had never smiled

they called her
the girl who never smiled

they called her names
to her face and some behind
she was always quiet
with her head down
in a book thousand
pages thick
until one day
another boy came to her
and a grin escaped
from the lips
of the girl
who had never smiled.

addiction

I have an addiction
to my phone
no, not my phone
but the faces in
the screen
smiling, crying, doing whatever
they can to entertain me

I don't remember
when I got this addiction
maybe it was the time
when I first saw her
face that was hundreds
of miles away.

whisper of the heart

I had fallen too deep
with no escape
and no matter
what I did
in the end
it was all
helpless against the
whispers of my heart.

antidotes and magic pill

maybe one day
the mighty scientists
will create a magic pill
that can cure all my
invisible illnesses

until then I'll take
you as my antidote.

young

she was
young when she
fell for a boy
who taught her
the only words he knew
the language of hate and neglect
she was young
when she fell for a boy
and she never loved another boy again.

old souls

maybe we are two
souls too old
in a time
that's become
too young.

vibe

you say
you like my
vibe but
I must warn you
it looks good
from a distance
but sometimes these
vibrations are a little
too much sometimes these
vibes are out of my control.

bittersweet

I'm bitter
like coffee
and need
just a little
bit of you
like sugar
to make me
better but not
too much
that I lose
my bitterness

first moments

learn to
cherish your
seconds and thirds
fourths and fifths
and the ones that follow

because the thing
about firsts
is there can
never be another first.

nomad

I fell in love with a nomad.
unfortunately, the thing about nomads is
just like they move from one place to another
so does their heart.

broken strings

and I play sad songs
on my out of tune
guitar battered
with broken strings
I play a broken melody

but to you it's
the best song
you have heard
for each word
and each string
is meant for you.

lonely barista

I met the
lonely barista
in the
café that no
one visited

she was
bitter on
the surface
holding a world
of sweet inside
her being.

a karaoke song

ours (love) was like
a karaoke song
by two clueless
birds singing in
a language
they don't speak.

love knocks

I had shut down
so many parts of me
I didn't know
which one
to open
when love
knocked
on my door.

Walk Forever

one step
at a time
we can do it
no cars
no rides
no lifts
no planes
no tickets
no buses
no help

let's walk
together
forever
we can do it

let's walk
and one day
we'll fly
away to
a better place.

all the hate you carry

all the hate you carry
is not enough
to fight all the
love inside of her

all the darkness
inside of you
is not enough
to put out
her fire

all the hate you carry
will never be enough
for she carries
a world of love
on her shoulders.

no more lonely lies

no more lonely lies
she said to the
lonely boy
maybe you'll learn
to let go for just
a little bit
just a little longer

no more lonely lies
let's talk in truths tonight.

run away

let's run away
without a plan
we don't need
a car or house
let's run away
and camp
somewhere under
the stars.

underwater

she only goes
to places
where the music
is loud enough
to drown out
the conversation.

seven years

it's been seven
years that
we had met
thought
I would have forgotten
it all
but your voice
your touch
your walk

I remember them
like a song.

a shack in the sand

you are like a beach
and its sunset
I am always on the edge
and you are the tide
that washes away
all my pain
you are like a beach
and its sunrise
I am far away from the shore
and you are my shack in the sand.

the hour that doesn't exist

it's the time
hours past midnight
hours before sunrise
even the insomniacs
have slept
and the dreamers
are yet to wake up

let's meet
in the hour
where time stands still
just for us
meet me
in the hour that
doesn't exist.

sweetheart

sweetheart
we are
the only
two planets
that bear life
galaxies apart
in a lifeless universe.

IV

A Lonely Generation

twenty-two

I am not lonely
I just check my phone
twenty-two times
to see if there is a new message

I am not lonely
I am just checking
to see if you have commented
on the picture I uploaded
twenty-two minutes ago

I am not lonely
I am just waiting
for someone, for anyone.

nature of evil

some villains
are scary
not because of how
evil, vicious, dangerous they are

some villains are scary
because how close they are to
being just like us.

lunar phases

there's a
moonlight like
sadness inside me
it comes and goes
in lunar phases
forever in the shadow
of a greater sorrow.

sanity

it is only
after I was
broken
I realised
how we
take sanity
for granted.

trust

I learned about
trust the hard way
when I was little
the only flowers I had known
were the one with thorns
the only rain I had known
was the one in a storm.

staircase

I'm hurt
and the pathway
to heal is a staircase
that never seems to end.

whole

and we pack
clothes, books
and toothbrushes
put all our lives
in little boxes
and move
to another town

and we
divide our souls
into little pieces
to put it in little boxes
and move to
another world

and we'll
never be
          same
never be
          whole.

naked

how can they know
what's it like
how can they know
what it's like
to be in fur jackets
but still feel naked?

smiles in photographs

they hate to be sad
so they put on fake
smiles in photographs
they share online

they hate to be sad
so they rewrite memories
in the stories they write

they hate to be sad
so they dance
to songs they don't like

they refuse to be sad
and that is why
they can be never happy anymore.

black and white filters

I put black and white filters
on colourful photographs
of the summer
I took with my polaroid

I put black and white filters
because I am afraid of
all the colours
all the details
and little imperfections
in the photos
of my world

I put black and white filters
not just on my photos
but all my life.

fifteen

It happened sometime in November
when I was just fifteen
and my life
was no longer mine
it belonged to the strangers
the singers and the dancers
I knew the names
but I didn't know the people behind
it belonged to the books and news
that were taught to me by the
writers and anchors

I knew how to read
but not how to understand

it happened sometime in November
when I was just fifteen
and my life
was no longer mine.

choice

she woke up one morning
wishing she didn't have to
choose which top to wear
and how to walk
on the road
to her office
with dozens of eyes
that belonged to faces
of strangers
who didn't know
who she was
what she has been through

she woke up one morning
wishing she didn't have to choose
how to live her life
for the sake of everyone else.

the photographer

he liked to
click photos
of birds on a wire
of landscapes
and woods and wolves

he was a photographer
who took photos
of empty streets, stadiums
and sunsets
he captured
it all, all except
photos of other people.

afraid

there were words
she was afraid to
speak out loud
afraid of what
they'll hear
and what they'll think
and what they'll say
back out loud to her

there were words
she was afraid
to say out loud
things she knew
in her heart to be true.

a generation lost

in just five years
a generation
of eighteen-year-old
                dreamers
have turned into
twenty-three-year-old
                lost souls.

suitcases

the first time I moved
to my college hostel
I realized how little
we need
when I could pack
my entire life
in three suitcases.

pocket watches

I wish
we still
had pocket
watches
isn't
it a thing
of beauty and magic
to carry time
itself in the palm
of your hands?

small windows

oh, how true it is
that the
smallest windows
in the world
hide the biggest dreams.

a rolling stone

I was once a rolling stone
never in one place
never in one heart
I rolled down
too far into
my own darkness.

always the wait

you know what they say
about the anticipation
being worse than the fall

I thought the rain
would come and
wash it all away and
leave nothing behind

that month I waited
hours and days for
the clouds to burst
for the storm to
thunder down
on our house

it eventually poured
but I was
already long gone
before the fall.

tap tap tap

thousands of taps
and double taps
and comments
trying to shape
and mould our
thoughts
trying to
tell us how
to think
and behave
until
everyone
everything
becomes the
one and same.

just hot water

are you a coffee
or a tea person
maybe I am neither
just hot water
that filters through
coffee beans and
tea leaves.

detectives

when did we all
become detectives
in our lives
looking for clues
of a case that can never be solved.

the first criminal

it took me too long
to realise
a detective
in a city with no crime
is doomed to become
the first criminal.

all the flowers

all the flowers
that I saw today
down on our earth
waiting to be
stepped upon
I took them all
and hid them
in my little notebook.

V

A Lonely Hope

where I want to be

sometimes it feels
like there's an
ocean between
where am I
and where
I want to be

sometimes I
sail on a ship
to cross the ocean
but there are
storms in my way

and sometimes
(though rarely)
I manage to reach
the lighthouse on the other side.

battle

maybe this battle
with just one soldier
shall go down
in history

like the ones in
Panipat or Bastille
where she fought
with herself
with the strength of
a thousand warriors.

fast car

maybe all that'll be
left in the end
will be our
long drives and
road trips to nowhere.

windchimes

some days I stay still
like the windchime
with no air

and some days I roar
like a windchime
in a hurricane.

mountaintop

every few days
I have mountains
in front of me
mountains so tall
they seem impossible
to climb

and every few days
I run walk and crawl
and somehow
reach the mountaintop

roads far far away

these days
I feel like
a hitchhiker
waiting for a
passerby
on a bike
or in a car
or a bus perhaps
that can
help me escape
to roads far far away.

it's okay

it's 2 am
and we are
in the middle
of nowhere
but it's okay

the car is
barely running
with its headlights
breaking the
pitch black nothing
driving down
an unknown road
but it's okay

it's okay
you are with me
and we are together.

plain old water

I have never
been the one
to drink or smoke
somehow
I found my intoxication
in plain old water and air.

songs of a time gone by

her brother
said let's forget the
world and listen
to the favourite
songs of our
mother together.

your city

and tonight
I am a stranger
in the city
you call home
and tonight
I am here
for a moment
where you
have lived forever
but tonight
you are with me
and I am here
to make this city mine.

make the moon

and maybe one
day they will
create a moon
on earth
just like the
one in the sky
and it would
shine just as
bright with
all its majesty
and imperfections
its craters
and dark sides

maybe one day
they will
make a moon
on earth
but
I'll still look up
I will always look up.

prisoner

I became the
unknown victim
of a soulless city
can you help me
escape to the wild
and see for the first time
the real stars in the sky.

olive

the window
in the train
calls to her
on the edge
of the seat
there is a girl
that looks far off
to the distance
to a girl in
an olive landscape
who looks back
to her
they are both the
same in different times
of their lives.

enough

enough telling
me I am special
and destined for
great things
you make me
believe
almost

I am not
meant to be
someone special
someone who
will change the world

I am ordinary
ordinary as they come
and that is special enough for me.

firefly in a jar

they have done it
finally captured me
in a glass prison
nothing but
a firefly in a jar
maybe I am
doomed to
look and light
the world outside
unable to escape

but I'll never let
my light go out.

it gets better

it's not how
it looks like
in the photos
and videos
through
tinted lenses

it gets worse

it's not how
it looks like
in the dark
lonely moments

it gets better

memories

how could I
ever be lonely
when the memories
of you are always by my side?

comfort food

when you are
down and out
and the whole
world seems
against you
the smallest
things can
be comfort food
a handshake
a hug
even
a conversation.

VI

A Lonely Poet

inspiration

I don't know
if it's a
blessing or a curse
to find inspiration
from tragedies.

letters

I write hundreds of letters
to my friends and family
thousands of flowy
cursive lines and words
I could never say out loud

I write hundreds of letters
just to put them in a box
with the rest of my thoughts

fleeting waves

she walked with grace
like a sea with
fleeting waves
but I wrote her
like a
relentless storm
on the page.

wrong turns

she thinks maybe
she was born
in the wrong generation
the wrong century
she took too many
wrong turns
in too many unknown cities
she could never belong to.

sad songs

she plays her
playlist of
sad and obscure
songs in the car
on a long highway
that leads to nowhere.

a single word

I wish that
every other
poem wasn't
about love
and every
other thought
wasn't about her
but here I am
thinking about her
writing a love poem
and I don't regret
a single world.

the anonymous poet

and I thought
I would be
the anonymous poet
wander through
the streets
and people
write poems
no city would
find and no muse
would read

but one day the
anonymous poet
was unmasked
his face
and fate
laid bare
to the whole world.

the everyday poet

maybe I don't understand
the meaning behind
every poem or story
and maybe some songs
go right over my head
and maybe modern art
is too modern for me

maybe I am just
an everyday poet
talking about
everyday things.

ink and paper

not all origins
have a backstory
of tragic tales
or marvellous miracles
no lightning in a bottle
no meeting of the stars

some of the best
origin stories
happen in the
simple moments of life
a walk down the street
a chat on the school bench

some of the best
origin stories
never find ink and paper.

saviour

when I was left alone
with my own thoughts
and a storm of darkness
and despair

poetry saved me.

fear not

glitter shines bright
but fades quick
these iridescent moments
will dazzle for a while
and disappear
but fear not poet
write away
words will remain forever.

magic

they promised
me a world
of magic
and awe
they left me
nothing but illusions
and heartbreak.

unwritten

let's not write
about the moon
or the stars
or the wild
and the wonderful
let's write
about the things
that no one
else will write about.

ghost writer

sometimes I feel
like a ghost writer
writing the story of
a million lives
that never had
the courage
or the opportunity
to write their tale.

sad poem number 7

this is sad
poem number 7
and I have
already written
six sad sonnets
in the past week

this is sad
poem number 7
and I hope
I can leave
some of the sadness
on the paper.

they found a way

they found a way
to turn all my
anxiety and sadness
into dollars and rupees

I never knew that
people could pay a lot
to see others in misery
but they found a way
to turn all this madness
into cheques and gold

and now all they want
is pain and loneliness
what choice do I have
but become the person
they want me to be.

I am not a book

I am not a book
for you to flip the
pages around

to pick it up from
the shelves
and go to
whichever chapter
you want

I am not a book
I am a journey
of which you
or no one else
has been a part of.

a single fan

it's him again
in the empty
stadium, arena, café
wherever he could find
for his fiftieth performance
to say his words
speak his story
with no one out
there to listen

if only there was
a single person
a single spectator
wander, fan
or follower
to push him through.

you've hurt me

you've hurt me
more times
than I count
until I had enough
and let you go

now you are gone
but I'll not write
a single bad word
about you

you've hurt me
too many times
but I'll turn
all that pain
to let the world
know all the
best parts
of you.

I fell in love with a city

I never realised
how dangerous it
was to fall in love
with a city

especially the big ones
with the high-rise buildings
and secrets buried
deep underground

a city with millions
it gave love to many
and destroyed many more

I never realised
how dangerous it was
no matter how
many sleepless nights
you spend in its streets
a city can never love you back.

last page

if you
write a book
about all you are
all you were
and all you are
meant to be
don't make me
the first chapter
or the ones
in between
but don't forget
to mention me
on the last page.

ABOUT THE AUTHOR

Himanshu Goel (born 18 July, 1995) is a software engineer, management graduate, poet and Indian author of five novels – 52 laws of love, A Rational Boy in Love, IRL – In Real Life, Tulsi and A lonely world, The Woman Who Saved my Life and other poems. He wrote and published his first book Tulsi while he was pursuing engineering at Punjab University, Chandigarh.

His short-form poetry gained popularity online through his Instagram profile (@lighthouse_foodie) and he subsequently published various poetry collections.